SONOMA STATE UNIVERSITY RUBEN SALAZAR LIBRARY

P9-DWN-098

This edition first published by Carolrhoda Books, Inc., 1984
Original edition first published by The Danish National Museum, Copenhagen, 1981
under the title TOBIAS FISKER FRA ISEN
Copyright © 1981 by Ole Hertz
English translation copyright © 1984 by Tobi Tobias
All rights reserved.
Published in agreement with International Children's Book Service, Copenhagen, Denmark
Manufactured in the United States of America

LIBRARY OF CONGRESS CATALOGING IN PUBLICATION DATA

Hertz, Ole.
  Tobias goes ice fishing.

  Translation of: Tobias fisker fra isen.
  Summary: In Greenland, a boy and his father fish
through the ice that covers a fjord.
  [1. Ice Fishing—Fiction. 2. Fishing—Fiction.
3. Greenland—Fiction] I. Tobias, Tobi. II. Title.
PZ7.H432463To   1984   [E]   83-26356
ISBN 0-87614-260-9 (lib. bdg.)

1   2   3   4   5   6   7   8   9   10   93   92   91   90   89   88   87   86   85   84

Tobias Goes Ice Fishing

by Ole Hertz

Translated from the Danish by Tobi Tobias

Carolrhoda Books, Inc.   Minneapolis

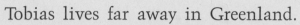
Tobias lives far away in Greenland.

He lives with his father and mother,
his big sister, and his little brother.

It is winter now.

The fjord is frozen over.

Today Tobias is going out with his father

to fish through the ice.

Tobias helps his father
take the ice chopper down from the loft.
They will use it to break a hole in the ice.

Tobias and his father walk out
across the ice that covers the fjord.
They pull a small sled behind them.

The hooks of their long fishing line
lie deep down at the bottom of the water,
but the end of the line is tied fast
to a block of ice up on the surface.
They set the line out yesterday.
Now they hope they have caught some Greenland halibut.

Tobias's father chops the ice
to open the hole and free the fishing line.

Now he begins to pull up the line.
He slings it over his shoulder
and walks across the ice,
away from the hole.
Then he lays the line down
and walks back to the hole.
There he picks up the line again
and pulls it out over the ice.
He does this again and again
until most of the line is up.
He pulls it in this way
so that he won't get too wet from the line and freeze.

It takes almost an hour to pull in the line
and reach the hooks.
That's how deep the fjord is.
Tobias's father must stand at the edge of the hole
to pull up the piece of line
where the hooks are attached.
He takes the halibut off the hooks.
He must do this with bare hands,
so his fingers get very cold.
Each time his father brings up a fish,
Tobias thumps it on the head with a piece of wood
so it will die.

Tobias puts new bait on the hooks.
On each one he puts a piece of fish,
something the Greenland halibut like.
Tobias's father looks up at the sky.
It has gotten dark.
That may mean bad weather is coming.
They had better hurry up and finish
so they can get home.

Quickly they pull up the end of the fishing line.
Now they will drop the line down again
with the fresh bait on the hooks.
There is a metal sheet at the end of the line,
called a glider.
It will pull the line down at a slant
so that the hooks will land on the bottom
in a long row,
not in a pile, one on top of the other.

Now the line is set.
Tobias and his father hurry home.
They wouldn't want to be out on the ice
if it began to drift away from the shore.
Tobias and his father reach home
just before the storm begins.

But they can't go inside yet.
First the fish must be cleaned.

Then Tobias and his father go to the fish house
to sell their catch.
Here the fish are weighed.
Tobias and his father are given
a piece of paper saying how much money they have earned.
Today they have caught 55 *kroner*'s worth of fish.

At last they get home.
Outside it has become completely dark.
Tobias's father prepares a new fishing line
while Tobias reads a magazine.
In a little while he will go to bed.

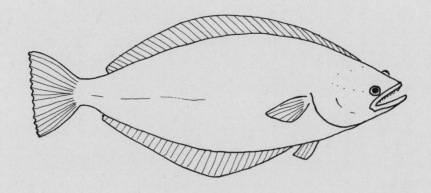

The Greenland halibut is a big flatfish, about 70 centimeters (28 inches) long. It lives at a depth of from 200 to 2,000 meters (660 to 6,600 feet). These halibut eat shrimp and smaller fish. They swim on their sides.

The halibut that are caught near settlements are either salted or frozen before they are sent on to fish processing plants in the towns. Greenland halibut are also used for dog food.